Caring and Sharing

Written and Illustrated by
Ron and Rebekah Coriell

Fleming H. Revell Company
Old Tappan, New Jersey

© 1980 Fleming H. Revell Company
All rights reserved.
Printed in the United States of America

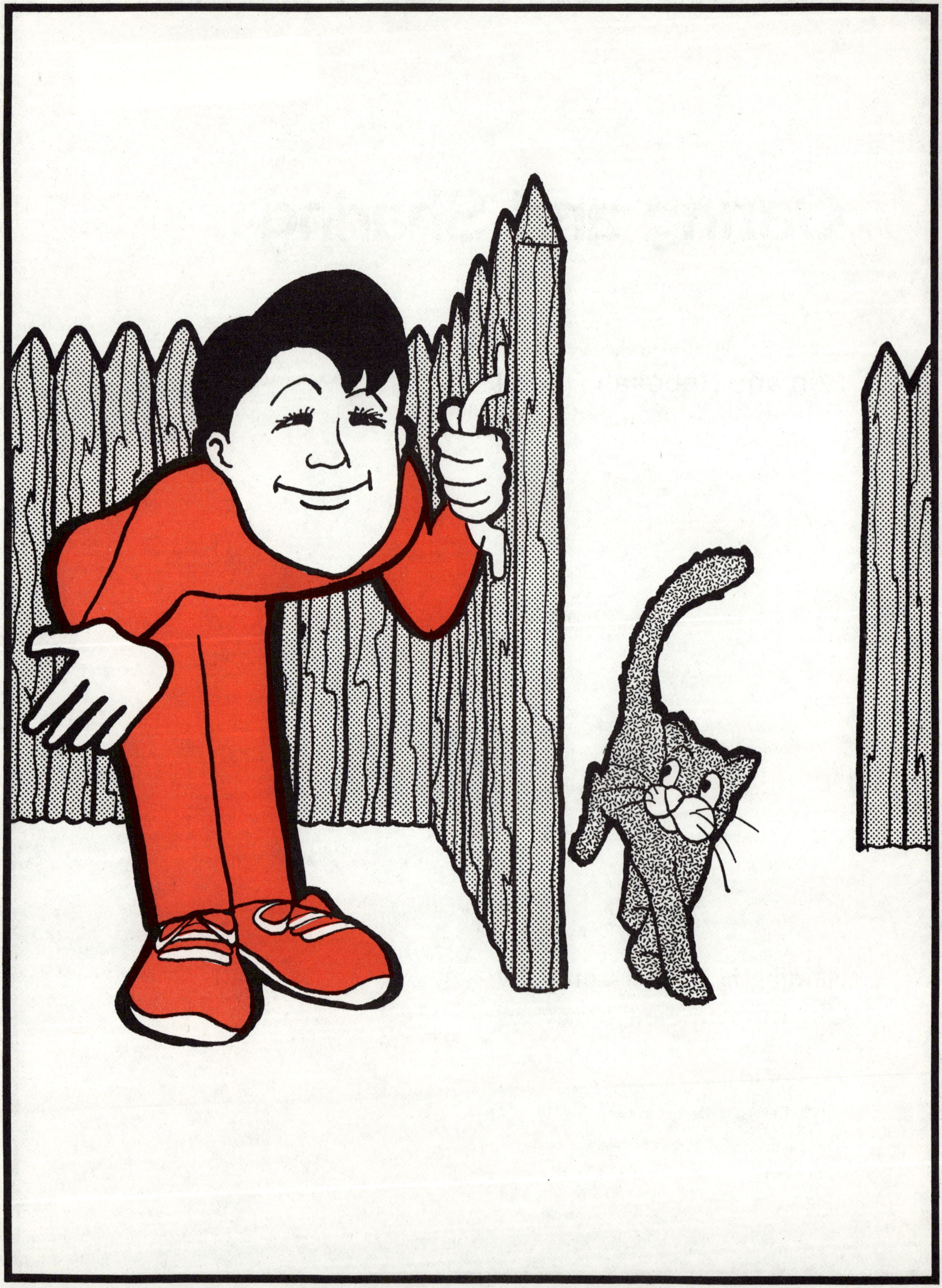

Initiate
gate

Making the First Move Without Being Asked

Go to the ant, thou sluggard; consider her ways, and be wise: Which having no guide, overseer, or ruler, Provideth her meat in the summer and gathereth her food in the harvest.

Proverbs 6:6-8

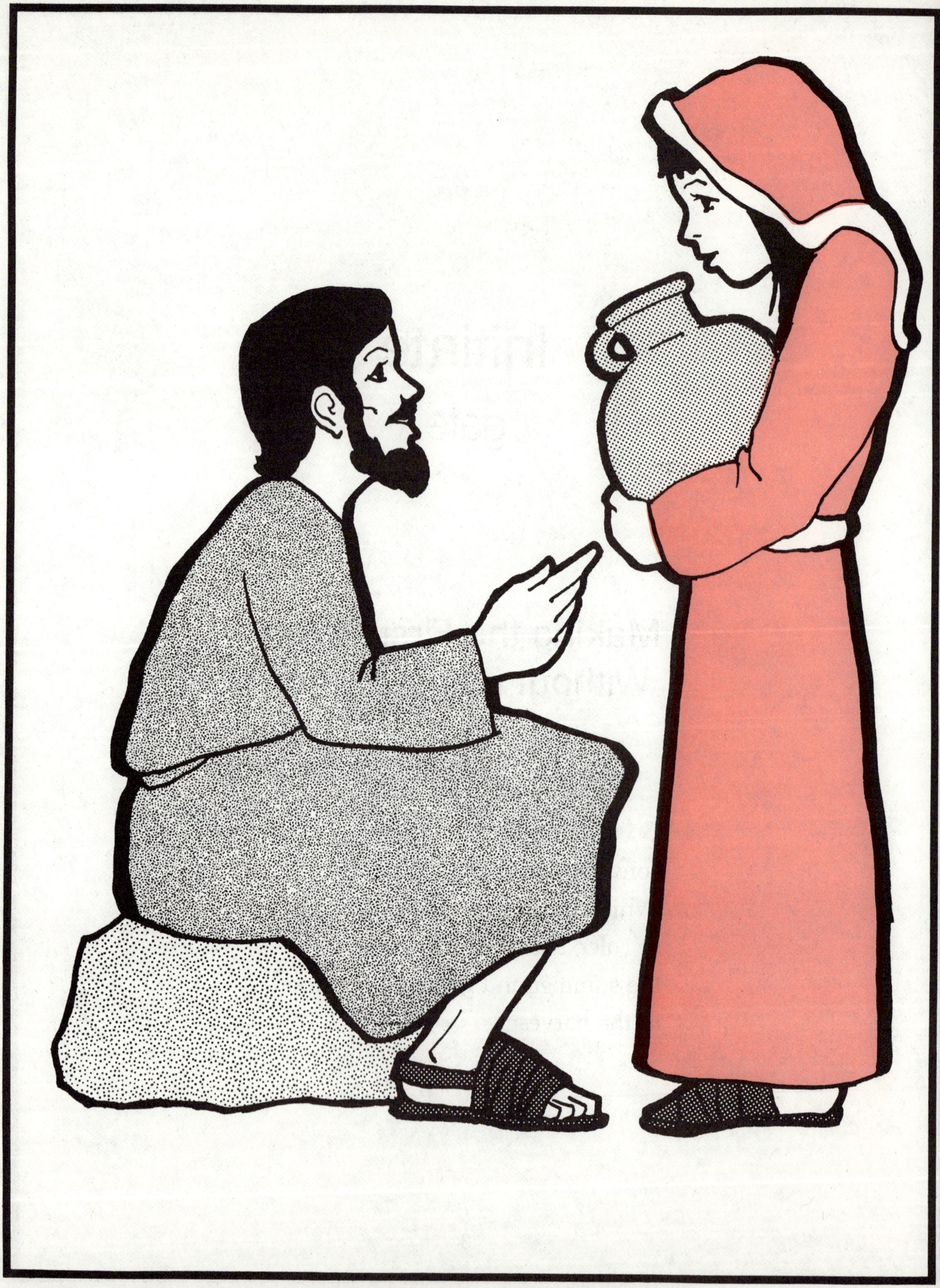

Initiative in the Bible

It was a hot midday when Jesus sat down at a well to rest from His walk. At the same time, a Samaritan woman came to the well to draw water.

In the land where Jesus lived, the Jews did not like Samaritans. They did not even like to talk to them. Jesus was a Jew, yet He took the initiative and spoke to the woman at the well. Because He is God, He knew that she needed to ask Him to be her Saviour.

She was surprised. She never expected a Jewish man to speak to her first. But, the more they talked, the more she realized that He was not an ordinary man.

She said, "I know that Messiah cometh, who is called Christ: when He is come, He will tell us all things" (John 4:25).

Jesus replied, "I who speak unto thee am He" (John 4:26).

The initiative of Jesus convinced this woman that He was no ordinary man. She later brought others to hear His teaching.

This story is found in John 4:5-30.

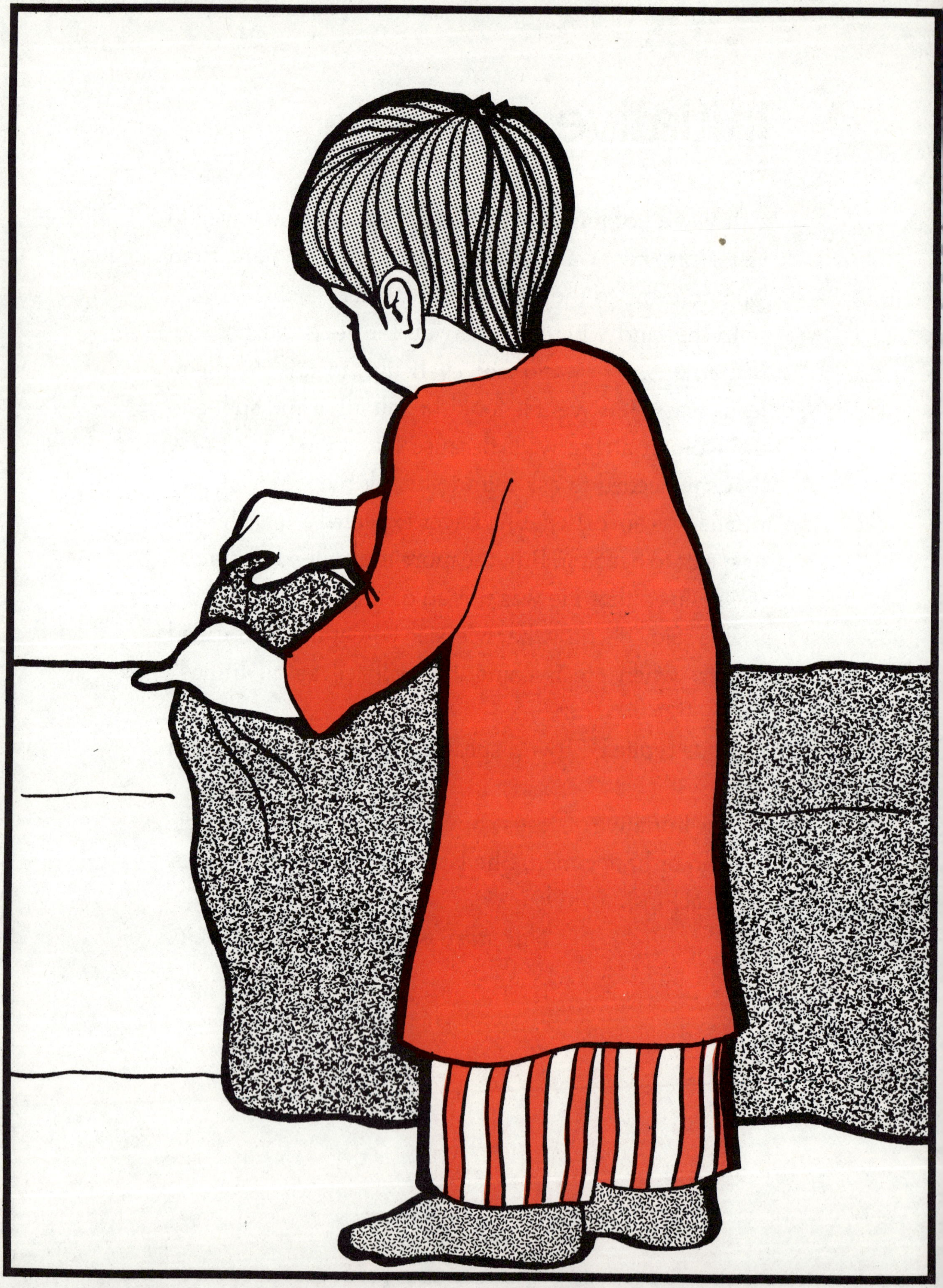

Initiative at Home

Adam pulled the covers over his head as Father's alarm clock rang. He and his family had been up late the night before and everyone was still sleepy. The alarm ran down without being shut off. One-half hour later, with one eye open, Adam looked at his own clock.

"It is late!" he shouted. "Mother, Father, we will be late for church! We have to get up now!"

Adam put on his robe and set out his Sunday clothes. He wanted to help the family get to church on time.

I know what I can do, he thought. *I will make my bed. Then I will surprise Mother and Father by making their bed, too. They will not have time to do it themselves.*

It took only minutes to complete these jobs. Then Adam washed his face, dressed, and came downstairs for breakfast.

Father had already noticed his son's kind helpfulness. "Mother," said Father approvingly, "we have a son who shows initiative. He made all the beds without even being asked. Thank you, Son. It will help us not to be late for church."

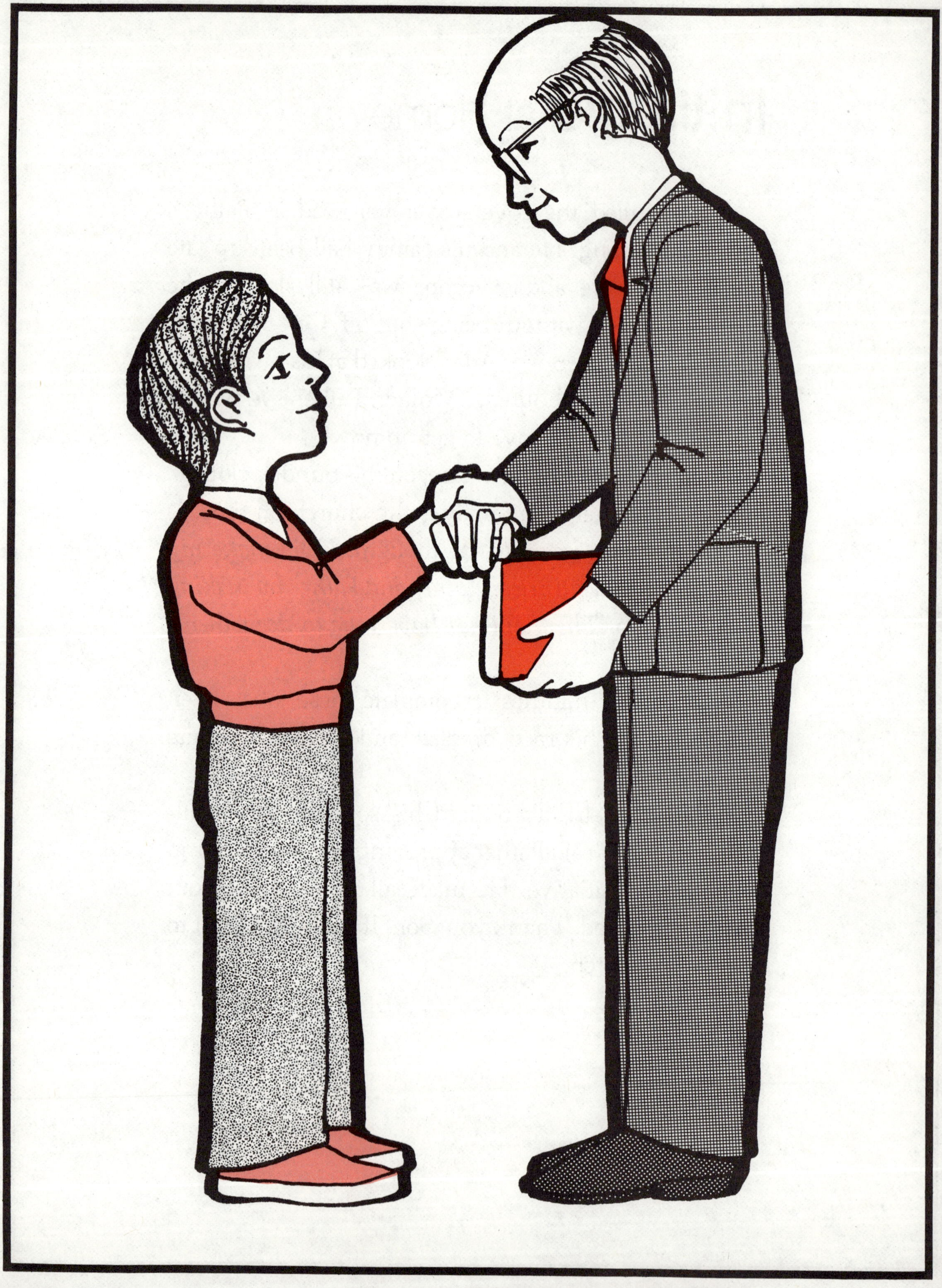

Initiative at School

Adam was hanging up his coat in the classroom when he noticed a book lying on the floor. It didn't look like any of the books used in his room. A paper clip was attached to the cover of the book. Adam opened the book and found a card, which read: "Whoever finds this lost book, please return it to the principal's office."

Adam tucked the book under his arm and went to his seat. He put it in his desk and took out his math book.

The school day was filled with many exciting activities. But all day long, Adam wondered about the note attached to the "lost" book.

When the school day ended, Adam gathered his homework and remembered to put the "lost" book in his schoolbag. Then he stopped by the principal's office.

Mr. King, the principal, greeted Adam with a smile. "I see you have found one of my lost books. Thank you for returning it."

"You mean you lost more than one book?" asked Adam.

"Oh, yes," replied Mr. King. "I purposely lost five books. I wanted to see who would take the initiative to return them to me. In return, I have a special award for you."

Adam was glad he had taken the extra effort to show initiative.

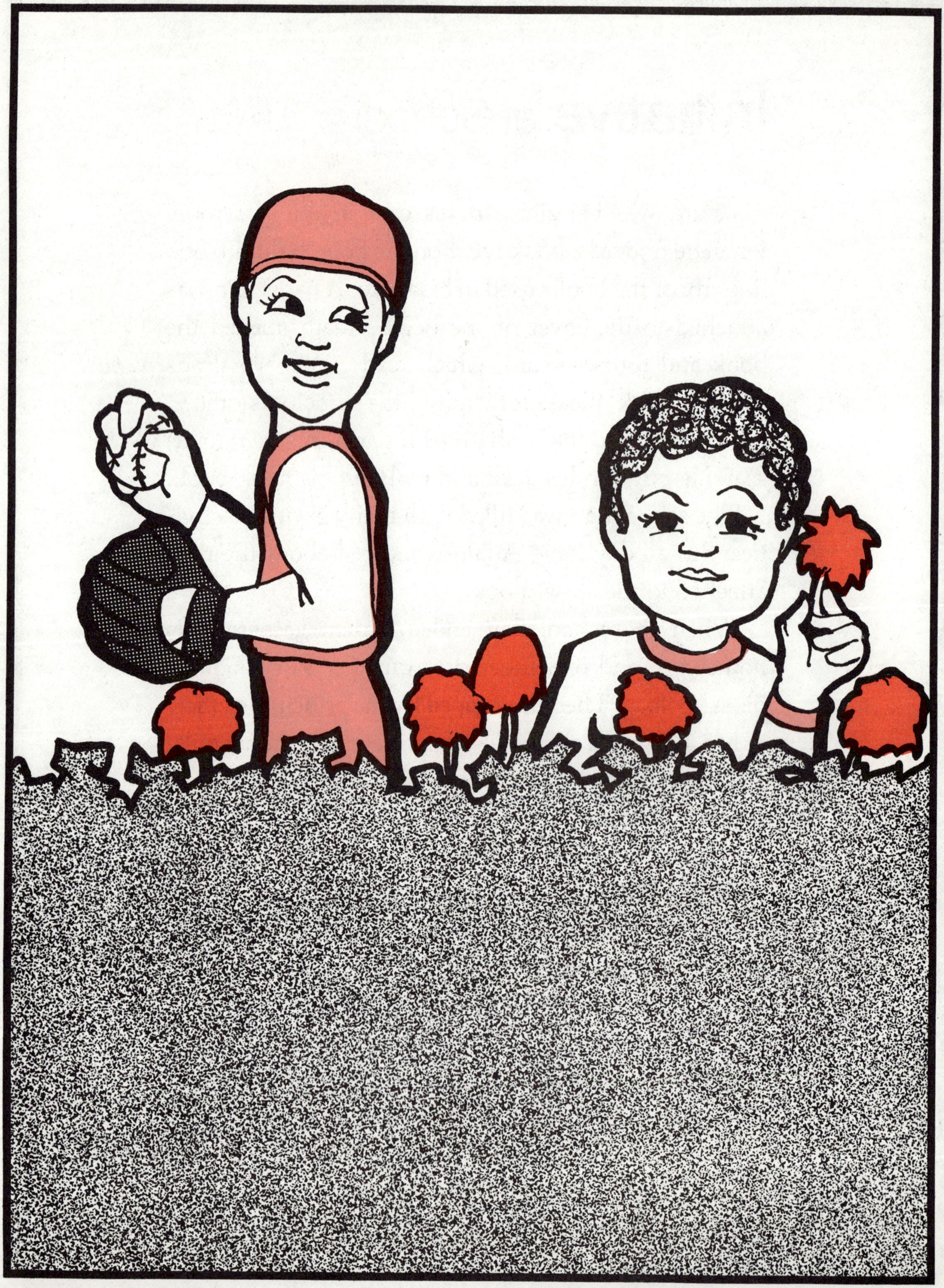

Initiative at Play

Adam Randall's backyard had the most beautiful flower garden in the neighborhood. His grandpa spent many hours lovingly caring for these plants. But Adam didn't pay much attention. He liked baseball better than flowers.

One sunny afternoon, while Adam and his friends were playing ball, Jeff, his little brother, began to pick Grandpa's flowers. Grandpa was lying on the porch swing asleep. Adam saw what his brother was doing, but he just didn't care to stop playing ball long enough to tell someone or to stop Jeff.

Later, Grandpa woke up and saw what Jeff was doing.

"Adam," he called, "didn't you see Jeff picking my flowers?"

"Yes, Grandpa," said Adam as he ran to him, "but I was too busy playing ball. I'm sorry it happened."

Grandpa looked unhappy. "Saying you are sorry doesn't put back my flowers. Jeff is too young to understand. You must use initiative. If you see him doing wrong, don't wait. Help him to do what is right."

Grandpa grew more flowers, and Jeff learned not to pick them. But, most important, Adam learned that when he knows how to do good, he must take the initiative and do it without being asked.

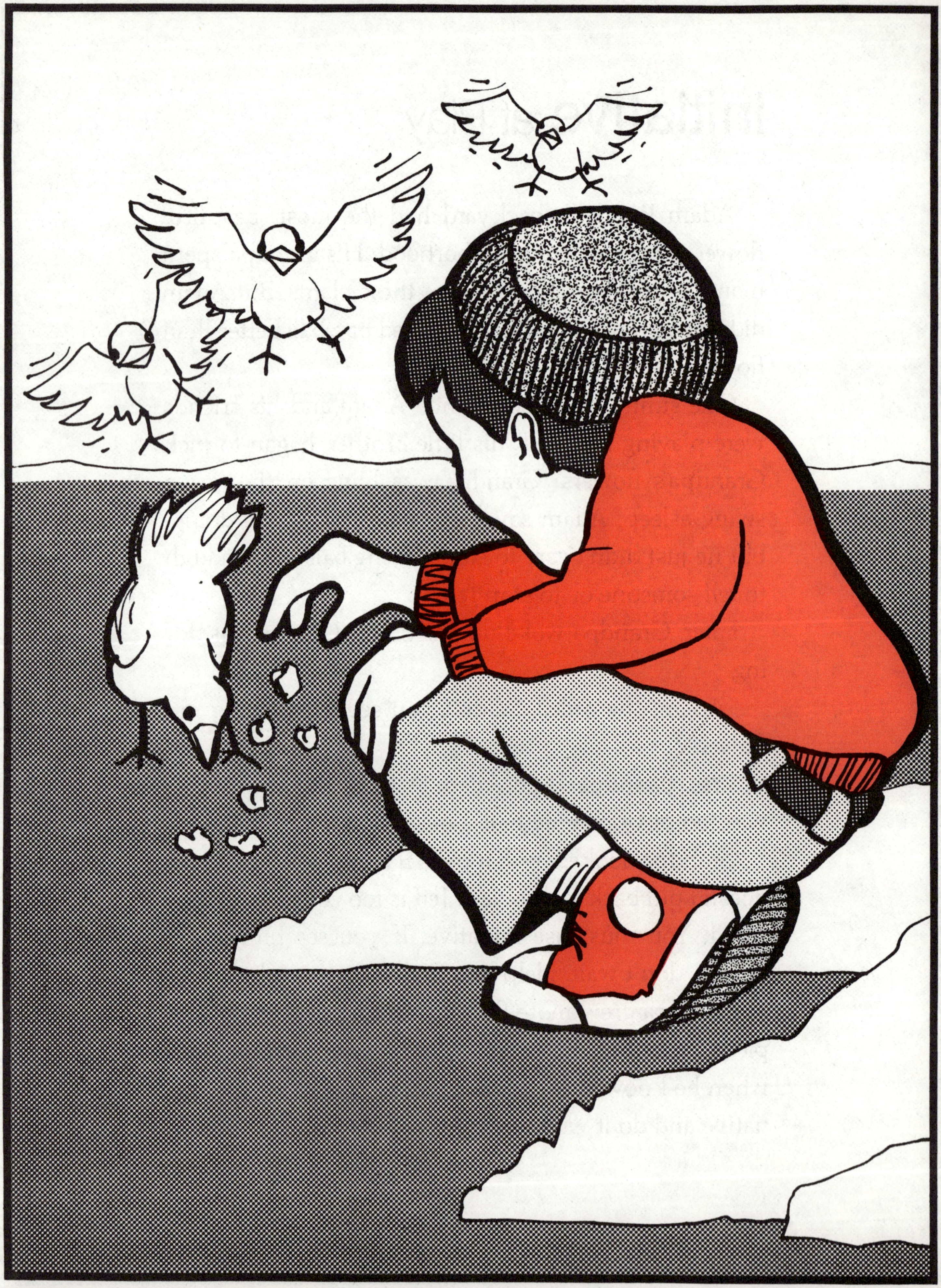

Love
dove

Unselfishly Meeting Another's Need

This is my commandment, That ye love one another, as I have loved you.

John 15:12

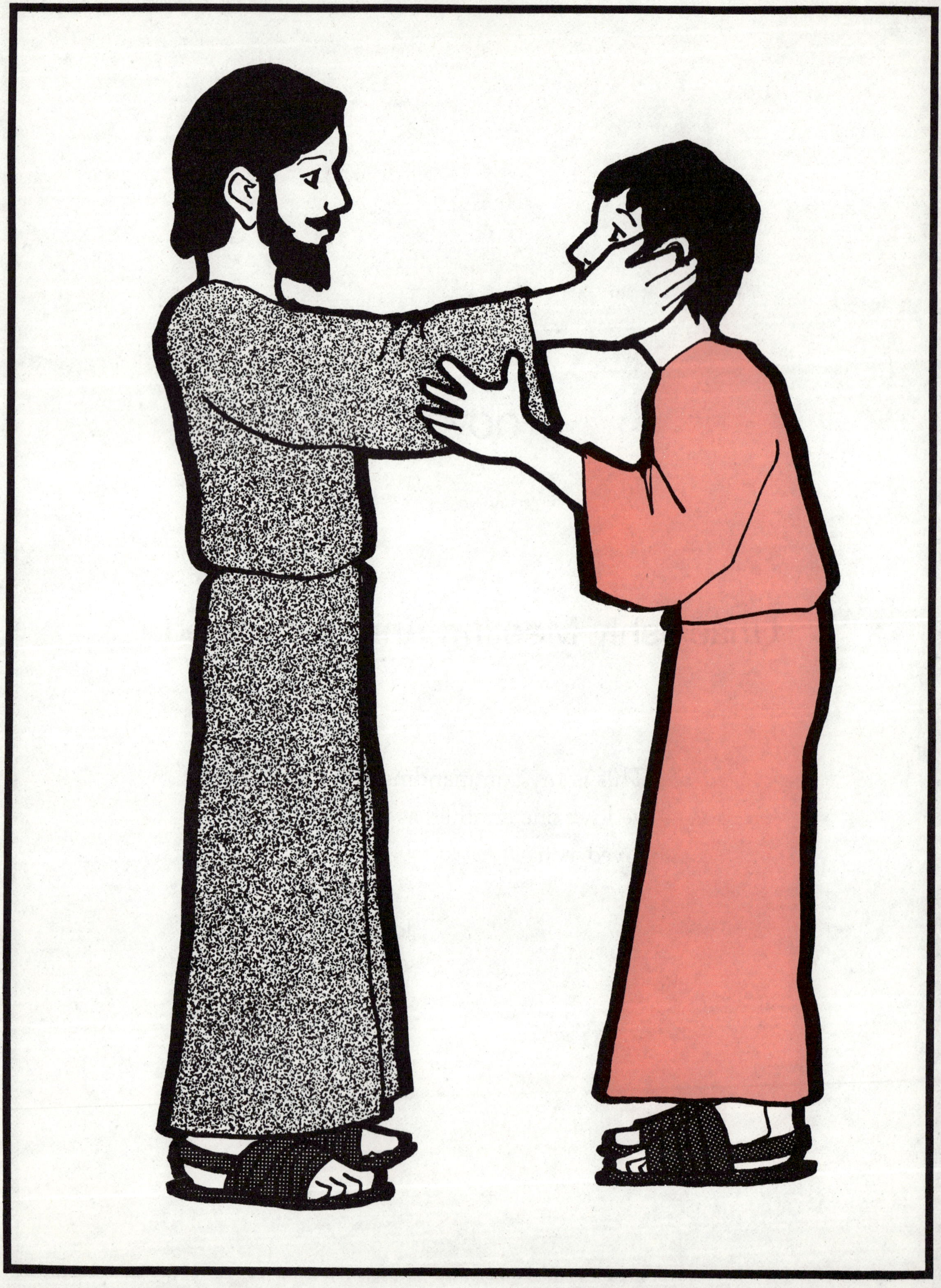

Love in the Bible

One day, while Jesus walked along a road, a group of people came to Him. They brought a man who was deaf and who had trouble speaking.

"Please, heal our friend," they begged Jesus.

As He looked at this man, Jesus loved him. He wanted to heal him. Meeting someone's need is the best way to show that you love him.

Jesus led the man a little distance from his friends. There He did a strange thing. Jesus put His fingers in the deaf man's ears. Then He spit and touched the man's tongue.

Looking up to heaven, He sighed and said, "Be opened" (Mark 7:34).

Immediately, the man could hear and could talk plainly. It was a miracle!

Jesus could have asked the man to tell everyone what a great healer He was. He would have gained much fame. However, Jesus healed the man because He loved him, not because He wanted to be famous. So He told the man not to tell anyone what had happened.

Jesus showed the man how truly He loved him. He healed him without selfishly expecting any reward.

This story is found in Mark 7:31-36.

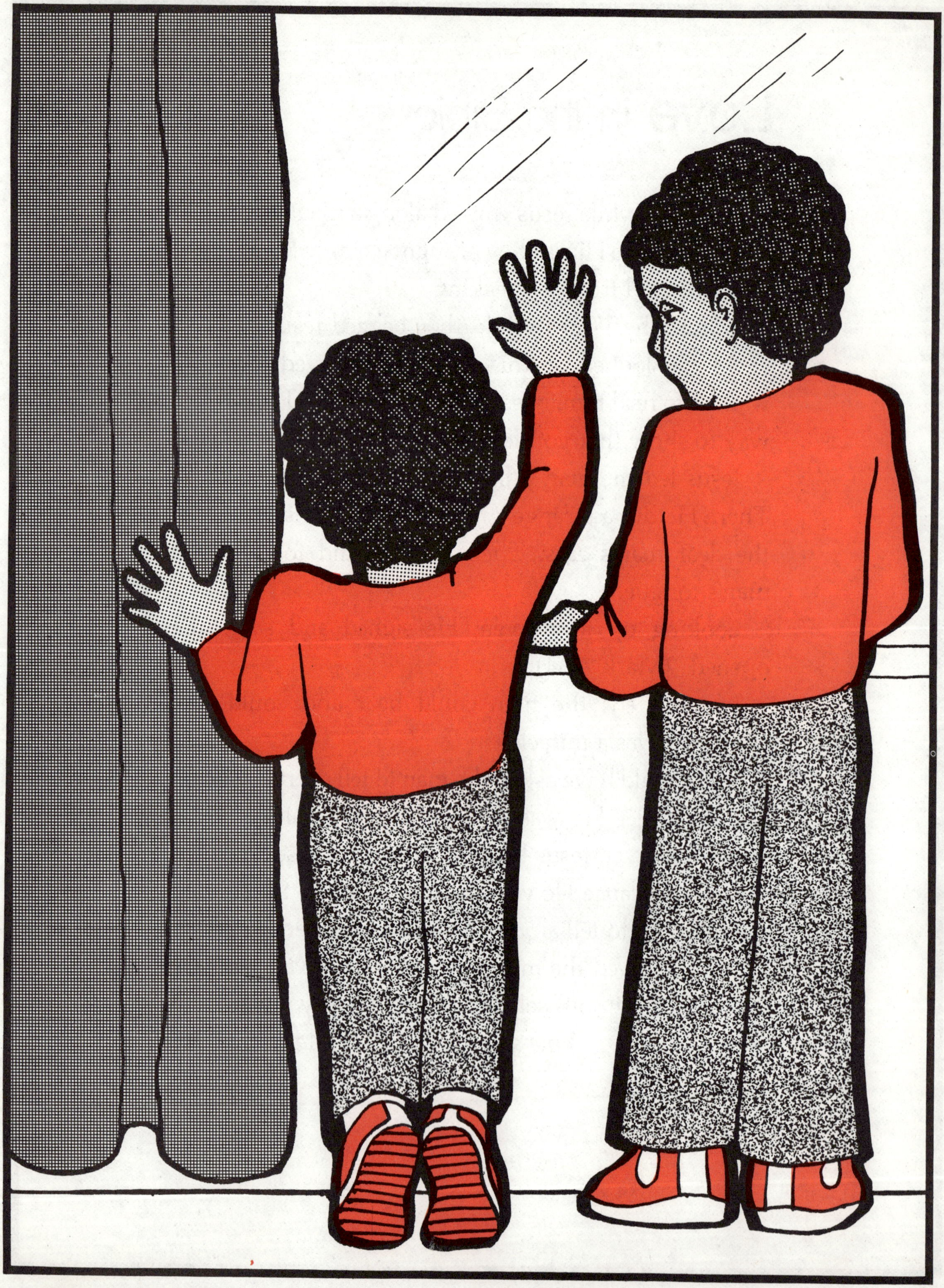

Love at Home

When his father was away from home on business trips, Roy missed him very much. This time, Roy could not wait for his father to return. He wanted to show him his report card. There was a great improvement in Roy's grades.

Davey, Roy's little brother, also missed Father. He was too young to understand why Father did not come home each night. After a few days, Davey became very lonely. He would ask Mother over and over again, "When will Father come home?"

Both boys ran to the picture window as they heard the familiar sound of Father's car in the driveway.

"Now I can show my report card to Father," Roy told his brother.

Davey yelled for joy, "Father, Father!"

Roy remembered how lonely his brother had been all week; he realized that Davey needed to see Father much more than he did.

Meeting someone's need is a good way to show that you love them, Roy reminded himself. *I love my brother more than any friend I have. So I'll let him see Father first.*

What a joy it was for Roy to watch Davey throw himself into Father's arms. Love was meeting his brother's need.

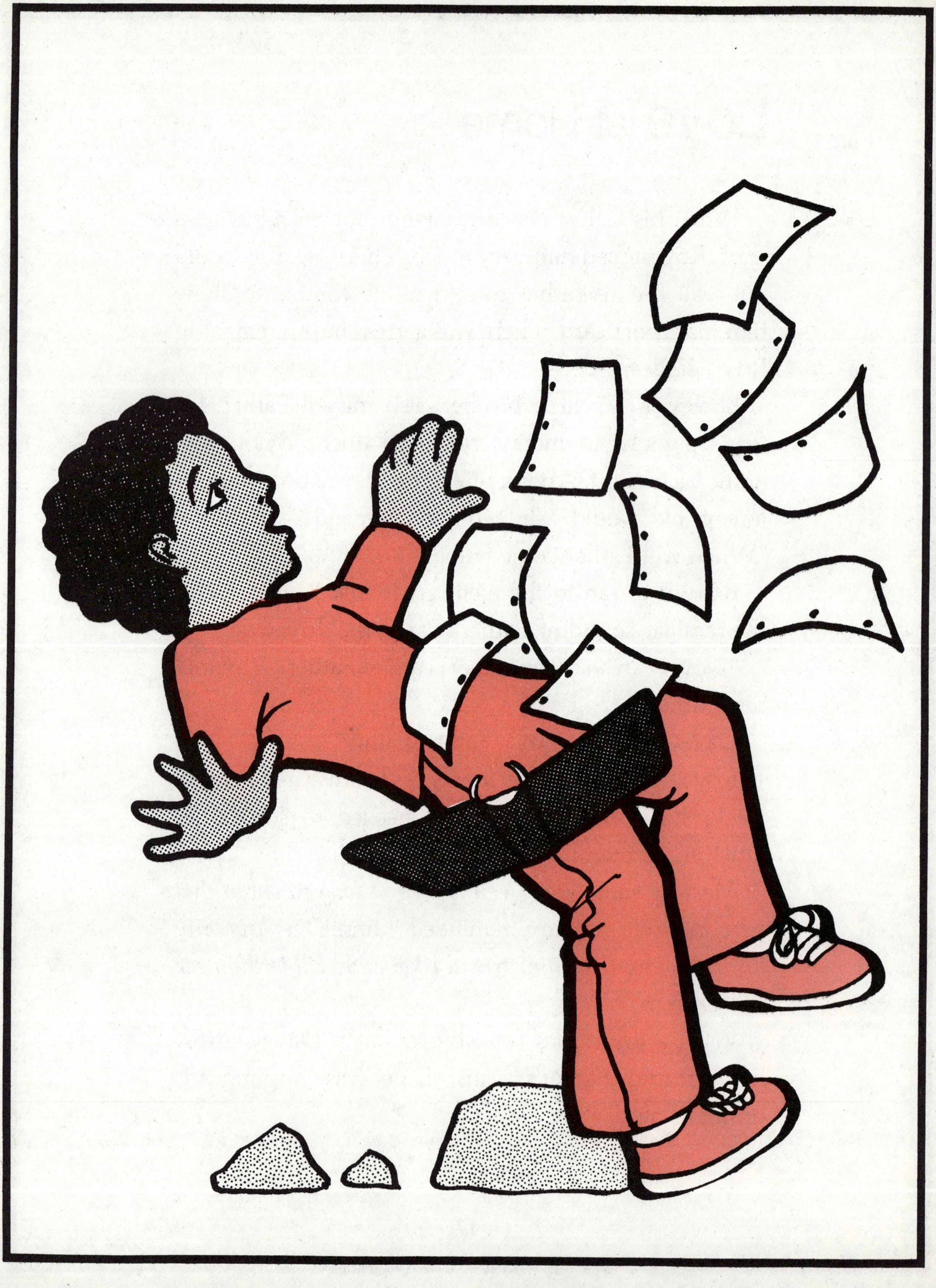

Love at School

The wind blew against the school bus. The bus shook. It was a windy spring day. As the bus rolled to a stop Roy and his friend, Terry, gathered their books and papers.

"Hold on tight to your papers and things," said Terry. "That wind is really strong."

Roy agreed and held his books tightly against his chest as he stepped off the bus. The wind was blowing so hard that he could hardly breathe. Finally he and Terry turned around and walked backwards.

They were almost inside the building when Terry fell.

"Roy, my papers!" yelled Terry as his papers and books slipped out of his hands.

Roy set his things down and immediately ran after Terry's papers and books. The books didn't go far, but the papers blew across the school yard, and pressed against a fence. There Roy and his friend were able to save them all.

"Thanks, Roy," said Terry. "I couldn't have saved my papers without your help."

"I was glad to do it," said Roy. "The Bible says we are to love our neighbors. To love is to meet someone's need, and you needed help."

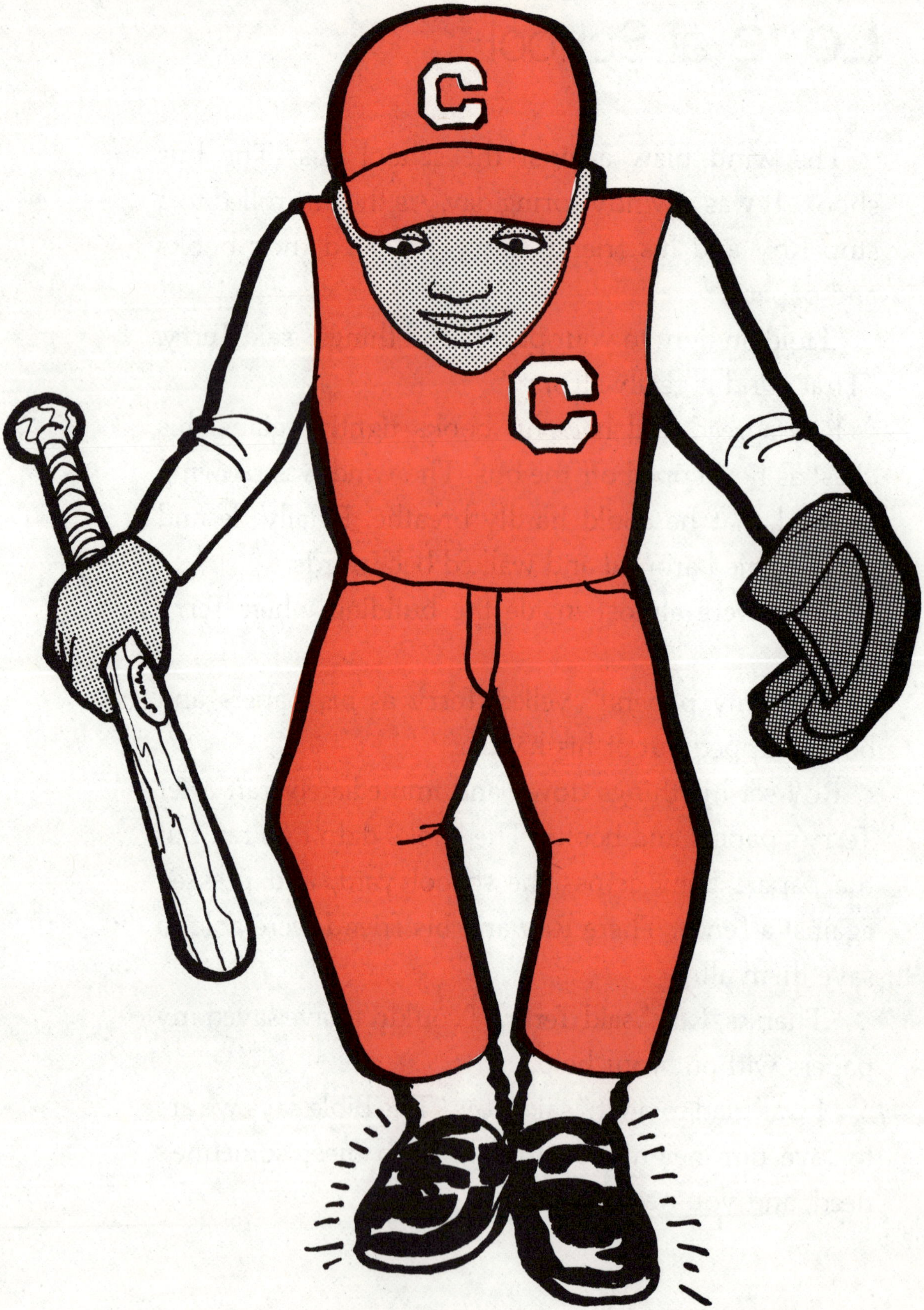
C
C

Love at Play

Roy could not wait to get home, change his clothes, and join his friends playing baseball. He rushed up the stairs, taking off his shirt and pants as he went. In less than five minutes, he had changed into his play clothes.

"Come on, Roy," a friend outside shouted. "The game is almost ready to start."

This made Roy rush even more. Down the stairs he hurried and out the door. He had almost run out of the backyard when he stopped. Looking down at his feet, he realized that he had forgotten to change his shoes. He was still wearing his good school shoes.

Oh, what shall I do? he thought. *If I go back to change my shoes, I'll be late for the game. But if I don't change, I'll be disobeying Mother.*

It was a hard decision for Roy to make. He thought it over before he decided. Then he went back to his room for his play shoes.

"What made you change shoes?" asked Mother, who had watched Roy trying to decide what to do.

"Well, I know you need and want a son who will obey you," said Roy. "And I love you more than baseball."

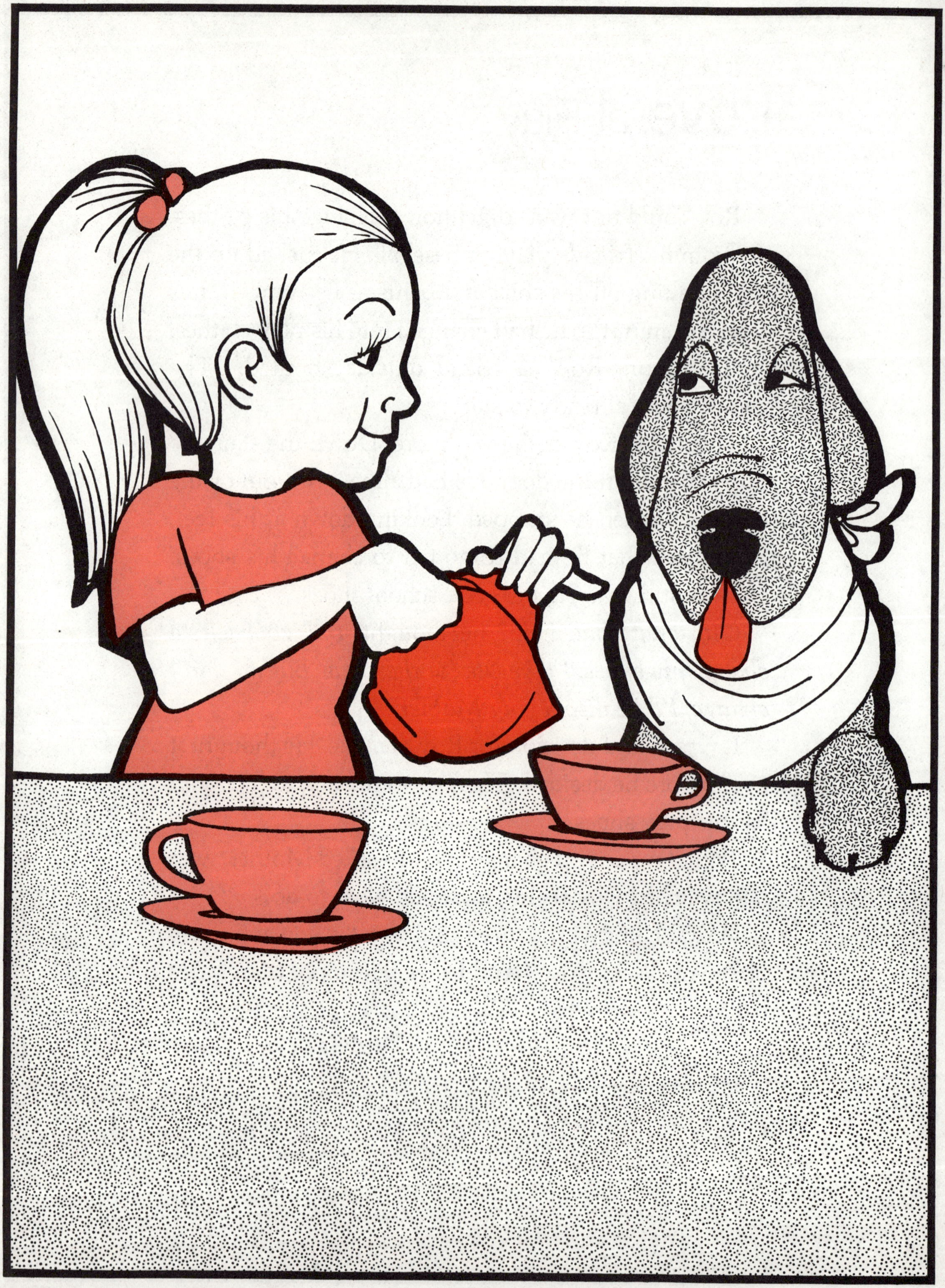

Generosity
tea

Sharing What I Have
With a Happy Spirit

Every man according as he purposeth
in his heart, so let him give; not
grudgingly, or of necessity: for
God loveth a cheerful giver.

2 Corinthians 9:7

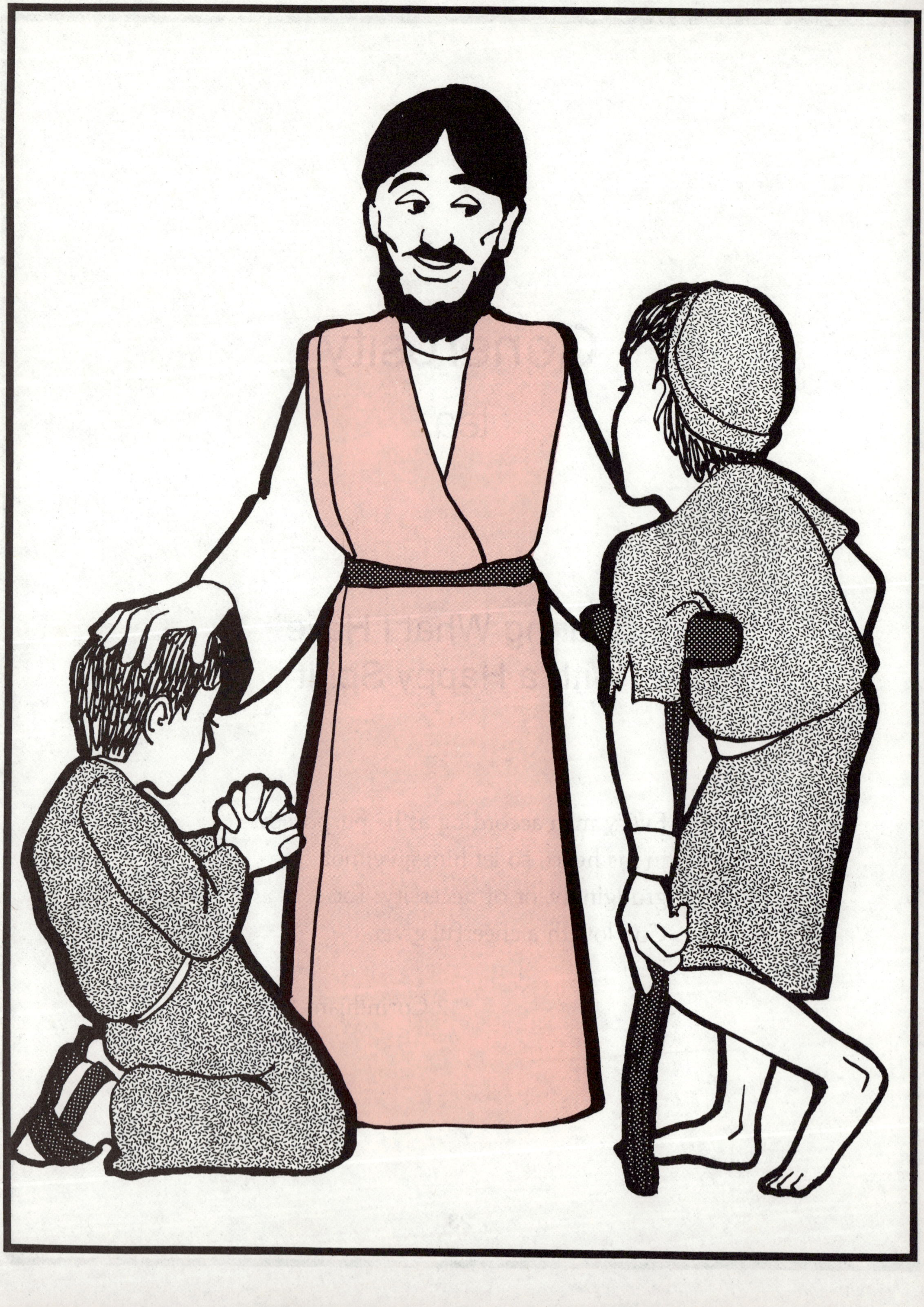

Generosity in the Bible

Jesus was a poor man. He did not own a house, a camel, or expensive clothes. He did not receive pay from working at a job. It would seem that Jesus had nothing to give to anyone else. One cannot share what he does not have.

However, Jesus was a very generous person. He shared again and again with people in need. He always did it with a happy spirit.

Jesus shared His healing power by helping Peter's mother-in-law get well. He once shared three days of His time to teach thousands of people on a mountain. Though tired from walking many miles, He still witnessed to a Samaritan woman by a well. He stopped to hear the cries of blind Bartimaeus and then healed him. Jesus took time to bless young children who were brought to Him by their mothers. He shared food and shelter with the disciples whom He had trained for three years. While at prayer one night, Jesus realized that the disciples were in danger as they sailed across a stormy lake. He quickly went to rescue them.

Jesus was indeed generous. Though He was poor, He did have wisdom, healing power, time, and love. These He shared freely.

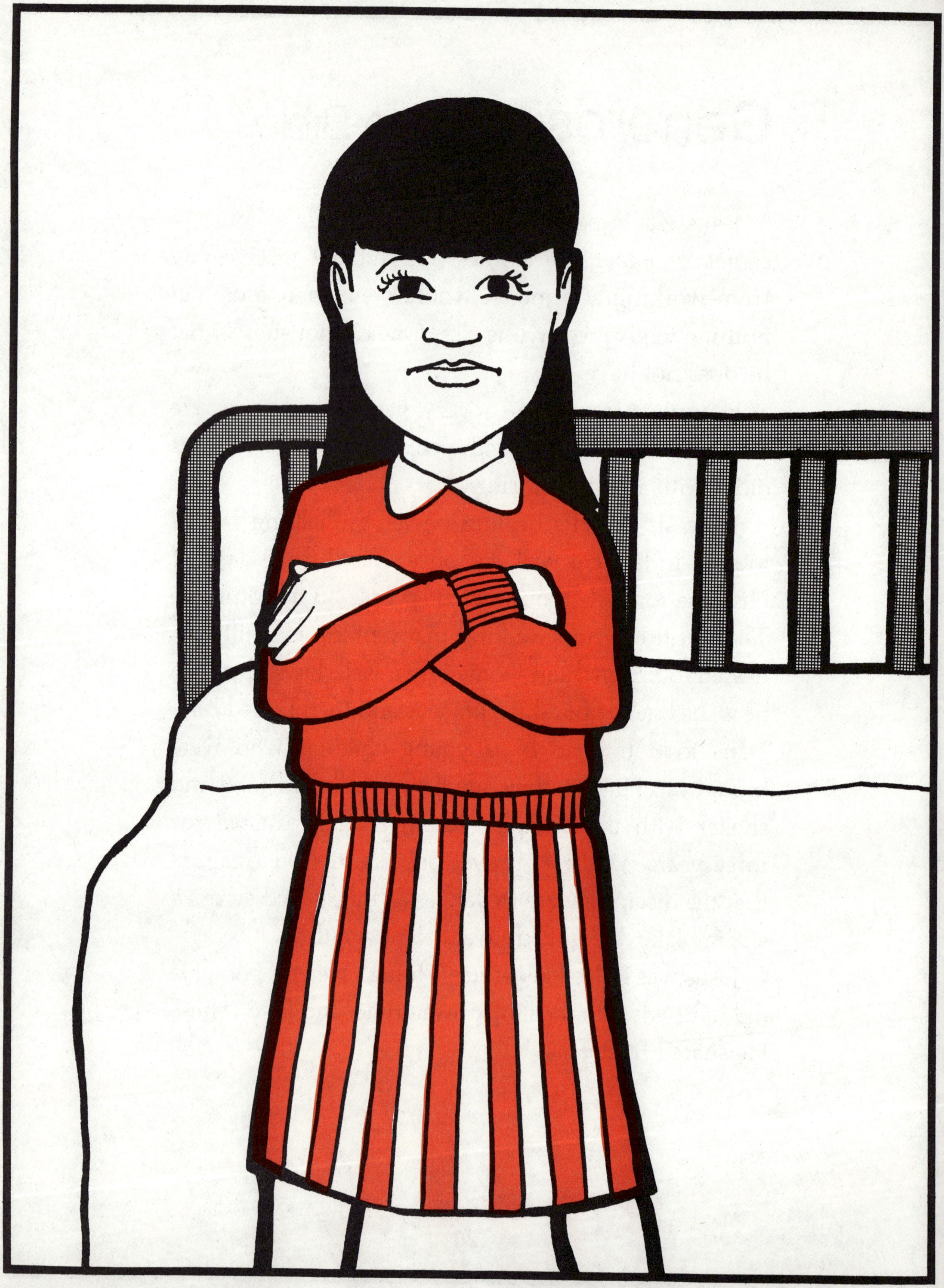

Generosity at Home

The Decker family enjoyed having missionaries as guests in their home. The missionaries would often come to their church to speak, and Mr. Decker would invite them home.

However, Sheri did not enjoy missionaries as much as the rest of the family. She always had to give up her room, so they could sleep in her large double bed.

"Mother, why can't missionaries stay somewhere else next time," pleaded Sheri. "I always have to give up my bed."

Mrs. Decker looked surprised and disappointed. "I'm sorry you feel that way. It is a special privilege to have these people in our home. Some of our missionary friends influenced your older sister, Laura, to serve the Lord in Africa. When we entertain them, they tell us interesting stories that you love to hear. And we discover what they need, so that we can pray for them."

Sheri paused to think about her mother's words.

"I had not thought of it that way," she said. "I feel better about giving up my room."

"I'm so glad," responded Mrs. Decker with a smile. "You are being generous when you share what you have with others, with a happy spirit."

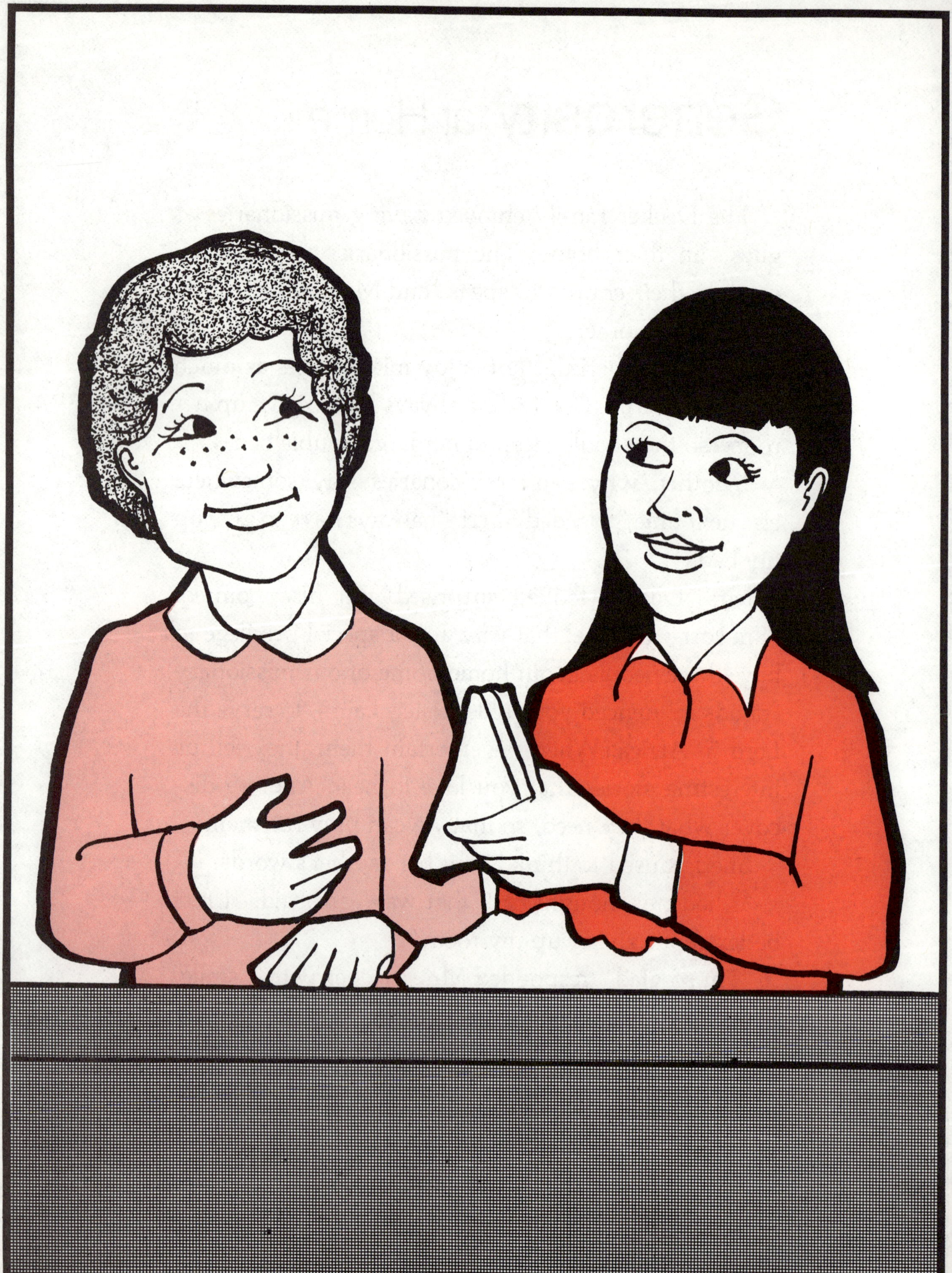

Generosity at School

Sheri's favorite lunch is a peanut-butter-and-banana sandwich, potato chips, and a carton of milk. She looked forward to Fridays with excitement. This was the only day her mother packed her favorite meal.

When the lunch bell rang, Sheri quickly put away her books and got out her lunch box. As she unwrapped her sandwich, she noticed that her friend Jill had a sad look on her face.

"What is the matter? Don't you like what your mother gave you to eat?" asked Sheri.

"I am sad because I forgot my lunch," Jill answered.

Sheri felt sorry for her friend. She thought Jill must be very hungry. It would be a long time until school was over. Sheri looked at her peanut-butter-and-banana sandwich.

"Here," she said, "you can eat half of my sandwich. And I have some potato chips to share, too."

Jill's face brightened. She eagerly accepted her friend's generosity.

Although Sheri ate only one-half of her favorite lunch that Friday, it was worth it. It made her happy to meet someone else's need.

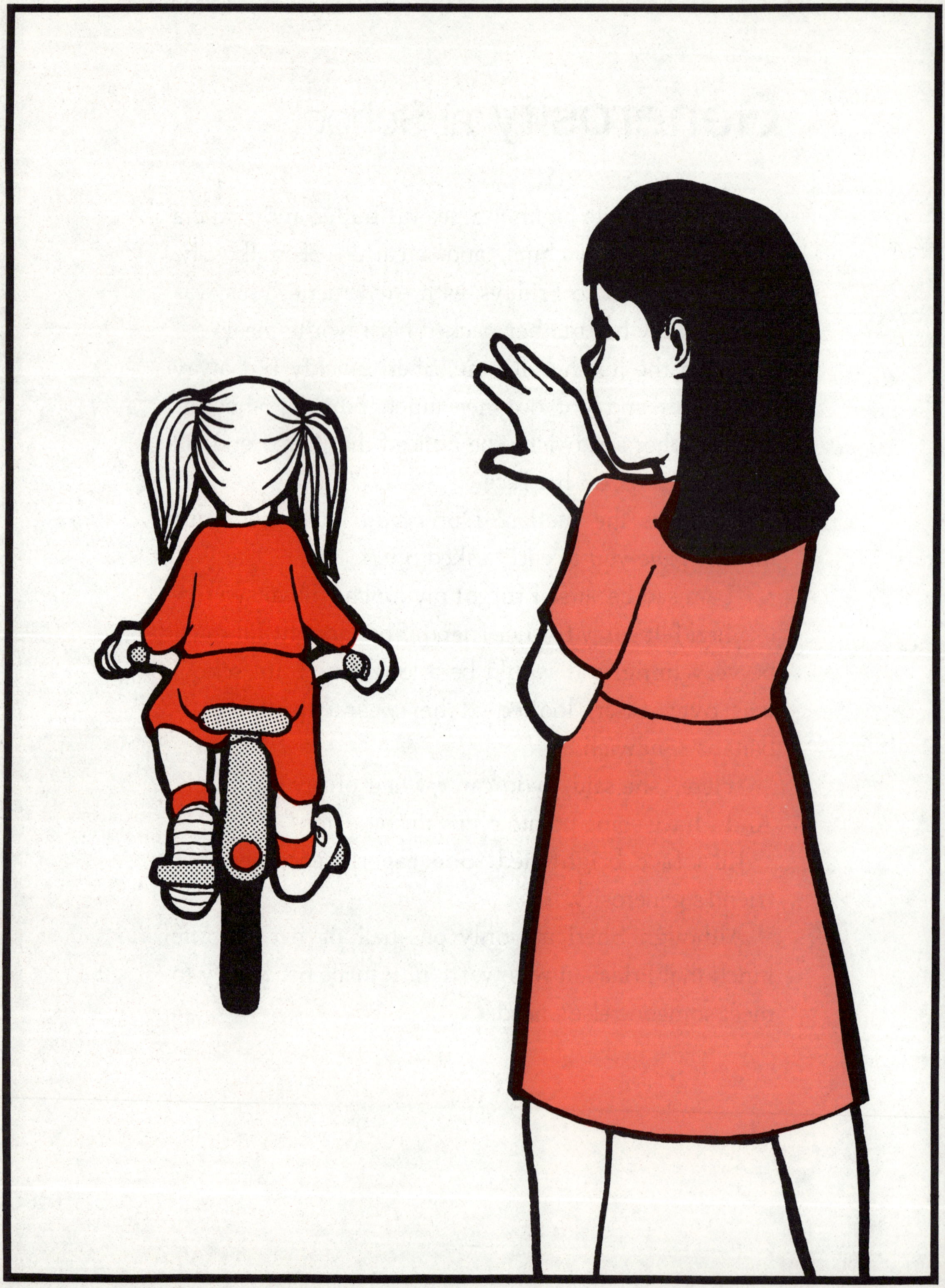

Generosity at Play

The new bicycle was bright in the sunlight. Sheri waited eagerly to ride it as her father finished putting air in the tires.

"Hurry, Father," she said. "I can't wait to ride the bike."

Mr. Decker was glad that Sheri was happy with her birthday bike. At last he finished, and Sheri jumped on and pushed up the kickstand.

"Here I go!" she called as she rode down the sidewalk.

Before Sheri had passed two houses, a friend ran up to see her new bicycle. Father watched the girls talk excitedly for a while. Then he saw Sheri get off and allow her friend to ride the bike. Up and down the sidewalk the friend rode while Sheri watched. Father paid close attention to see if Sheri minded that her friend rode so long.

Later, Mr. Decker spoke to Sheri. "I want to tell you how happy I am that you are a generous girl. I watched you as you let someone else ride your new bike. You shared with a happy spirit."

Character Development Challenges

This page is designed to give parents and teachers practical suggestions for teaching character traits to children.

Initiative

1. The child should think of three ways to help his father during the week and do the tasks without telling anyone.
2. The child should memorize James 4:17, to encourage initiative.
3. The child should ask a grandparent or older person how he showed initiative as a child.

Love

1. The child should memorize Mark 12:30, 31. Have him use these motions when reciting the verse:

   Heart — draw a heart in the air
   Soul — point to his chest
   Mind — point to his head
   Strength — flex his arm muscles
   Neighbor — point to others
   Thyself — point to himself

2. Using Psalms 116:1 as an example, have the child write a psalm stating why he loves God: "I love the Lord because _____."
3. The child should find a way to use his hands and his feet to show love, and his tongue to speak love to someone.

Generosity

1. Start a tradition in your home by using your child's birthday as an opportunity for him to give a present to his birthday guests, brothers, or sisters.
2. The child should compile a list of Bible characters who were givers (generous) and takers (selfish).
3. Have the child list ways in which he could be generous:
   I will give my time to help _____ .
   I will let _____ use my favorite toy.
   I will share my _____ with _____ .
   I will cheerfully give _____ to the Lord.